MARSEILLE TRAVEL POCKET GUIDE

Conseils de voyage à Marseille

SK TRAVELWITNESS

ISBN: 979-8-8505-5370-8 (Paperback)

All text, illustrations, and editing work were completed by SK Travelwitness.

First printing edition 2023.

MARSEILLE TRAVEL POCKET GUIDE

Experience the enchantment of Marseille | Unlock the Charm and Hidden Gems of the City Everything you Need to Know Before You Plan a Trip to Marseille

SK TRAVELWITNESS

TABLE OF CONTENTS

DISCLAIMER

While every effort has been made to ensure the accuracy and reliability of the information provided in this book, "Marseille Travel Pocket Guide: Experience the Enchantment of Marseille," we would like to emphasize that travel is inherently subjective and ever-evolving. The contents of this guide are based on research, personal experiences, and recommendations at the time of publication.

The writer of this book has purposefully made the decision to omit any visual descriptions, enabling you, the reader, to delve deeply into the realms of your imagination. By intentionally withholding visual imagery, the author aims to craft an immersive journey where you can personally explore the captivating locales and experiences of Marseille, untainted by preconceived notions or visual prompts.

However, it is important to note that the dynamic nature of travel destinations means that certain information, such as operating hours, prices, or policies, may change without prior notice. We encourage readers to verify any details with relevant authorities or establishments before relying on the information provided in this guide.

Furthermore, travel experiences are unique to each individual, and the recommendations and suggestions offered in this book may not cater to every traveler's preferences or circumstances. We encourage readers to exercise their own judgment and adapt the information to suit their needs, interests, and safety considerations.

The authors, publishers, and contributors of "Marseille Travel Pocket Guide" cannot be held responsible for any loss, injury, inconvenience, or damage resulting from the use of this guide. Readers are responsible for their own safety and should exercise caution while exploring Marseille or engaging in any activities recommended within this book.

Lastly, please be aware that travel regulations, local customs, and conditions can change over time. It is the reader's responsibility to stay informed about the latest travel advisories, guidelines, and restrictions applicable to their destination.

Travel with an open mind, embrace the unexpected, and let this guide enhance your journey to Marseille. We hope it serves as a valuable resource, inspiring you to create unforgettable memories while exploring the magic of the Marseille city.

INTRODUCTION

Nestled on the picturesque Mediterranean coast, Marseille beckons travelers with its irresistible charm, rich history, and a vibrant tapestry of cultural wonders.

This meticulously crafted guide is your key to unlocking the secrets of Marseille, offering an immersive experience that goes beyond the surface. Whether you're a curious adventurer or a seasoned explorer, our book is a compass that will navigate you through the labyrinthine streets, revealing the insider treasures that make Marseille truly extraordinary.

Prepare to be enchanted as you delve into the heart and soul of Marseille. Immerse yourself in the vivid colors and fragrant aromas of the local markets, where the tantalizing scents of lavender, freshly baked baguettes, and sun-ripened tomatoes fill the air. Indulge your senses in the Provençal flavors of bouillabaisse, sip on velvety wines produced in the nearby vineyards, and experience the gastronomic delights that define Marseille's culinary scene.

Beyond its culinary prowess, Marseille boasts a rich historical legacy that unfolds with every step you take. Marvel at the ancient grandeur of the Basilique Notre-Dame de la Garde, standing sentinel over the city and offering breathtaking panoramic views. Discover the secrets of the Vieux Port, where the echoes of seafaring tales still resonate, and witness the convergence of past and present in the contemporary architecture that graces Marseille's skyline.

But it is the people of Marseille who truly make this city come alive. Unveiling their warm hospitality, they welcome you with open arms, eager to share their stories, traditions, and cherished local haunts. Our guide opens doors to authentic encounters and invites you to embrace the vibrant spirit of this dynamic city.

Let our pocket guide be your trusted companion, leading you through the bustling streets and hidden enclaves of Marseille. With practical insights, insider tips, and carefully curated itineraries, we ensure that every moment of your journey is filled with wonder and delight. Whether you're seeking cultural immersion, outdoor adventures, or simply a rejuvenating escape by the azure waters of the Mediterranean, Marseille has it all—and our guide unveils it for you.

Unforgettable memories await you in Marseille, and our pocket guide is your passport to an extraordinary experience. So, pack your bags, unleash your wanderlust, and let the magic of Marseille guide you towards a journey of a lifetime.

CHAPTER ONE

INTRODUCTION TO MARSEILLE

Marseille, France, is a city that mesmerizes visitors and creates lasting impressions. As the second-largest city in France, Marseille offers a diverse range of experiences that are ready to be explored.

Beyond the city's boundaries, natural wonders abound. Marseille is blessed with stunning coastal landscapes that will leave you breathless. From the rugged Calanques, with their steep limestone cliffs and crystal-clear turquoise waters, to the idyllic beaches that invite relaxation and sun-soaked bliss, nature enthusiasts will find their sanctuary here. Hike along coastal trails, embark on boat excursions, or simply bask in the Mediterranean sunshine—it's a paradise for outdoor enthusiasts.

Marseille is a city that has it all—an enchanting blend of history, culture, natural beauty, and culinary delights. Whether you're in search of an immersive cultural experience, a romantic retreat, or an adventurous getaway, Marseille guarantees to satisfy your cravings and fulfill your desires.

The Culture and History of Marseille

Marseille has a rich historical heritage that spans numerous millennia, positioning it among the most ancient cities in Europe. Its establishment dates back to approximately 600 BC when it was founded by the Greeks under the name of Massalia. In a short span of time, Massalia prospered and grew into a prominent center for commerce in the Mediterranean region.

In the era of Roman rule, Marseille transformed into a notable Roman colony and played a pivotal part in the expansion of the Roman Empire. The city experienced remarkable prosperity both economically and culturally, witnessing the creation of impressive landmarks and the flourishing of various industries.

Throughout its long history, Marseille encountered numerous obstacles and underwent periods marked by invasions, conflicts, and shifts in political leadership. It came under the rule of different forces, such as the Visigoths, Ostrogoths, Franks, and Moors. Despite facing these turbulent times, Marseille demonstrated its tenacity and managed to retain its distinctive character, emerging as a resilient city.

During the 19th century, Marseille experienced notable industrial growth and evolved into a pivotal hub for maritime trade and ship construction. The city's port assumed a critical role in linking France with its colonies and facilitating global commerce.

Marseille's past is characterized by successive waves of immigration, particularly from North Africa, Italy, and various regions of Europe. This influx of diverse cultural influences has played a significant role in shaping the city's distinct character and fostering a vibrant multicultural atmosphere.

In recent times, Marseille has undergone revitalization initiatives and urban redevelopment, resulting in its transformation into a contemporary metropolis while simultaneously preserving its historical sites. Presently, the city serves as a living testament to its illustrious heritage, with traces of ancient Greek and Roman architecture still visible, including the renowned Basilique Notre-Dame de la Garde and the Roman Docks.

Marseille's rich history is not only evident in its architecture but also in its traditions, festivals, and thriving cultural landscape. The city takes great pride in commemorating its heritage through various events, such as the Marseille Provence European Capital of Culture in 2013, which served as a platform to showcase its artistic and historical significance to a global audience.

As Marseille continues its journey of transformation, it maintains a strong connection to its origins, paying homage to its past while embracing the opportunities and complexities of the present. The historical aspect of the city is a fundamental element of its appeal, enchanting tourists from around the world who are enthusiastic about exploring its rich blend of stories, cultures, and civilizations.

CULTURE

Marseille's culture is a captivating mosaic of influences that have molded the city's character and added to its lively and varied ambiance. From its ancient origins to its contemporary manifestations, the cultural fabric of Marseille encompasses a diverse array of elements, including customs, artistic expressions, music, gastronomy, sports, and the distinct lifestyle of its inhabitants.

Marseille's cultural legacy is intricately linked to its historical roots. Being among Europe's ancient cities, Marseille has been molded by a series of civilizations that have made it their home over time. Its inception as the Greek colony of Massalia, subsequent Roman governance, and later interactions with diverse Mediterranean cultures have imprinted a lasting impact on the city's customs and traditions.

The Mediterranean lifestyle plays a prominent role in Marseille's culture. Situated along the stunning coastline, the city has developed a strong affinity for the sea and a penchant for outdoor pursuits. The residents of Marseille embody a relaxed and unhurried mindset, cherishing the simple joys of life and relishing the abundant sunshine that graces the region.

The cultural scene in Marseille is vibrant and diverse, offering a wealth of artistic expression that weaves together into a colorful fabric of creativity. The city boasts an abundance of museums and art galleries that exhibit a wide range of artistic works spanning various eras and artistic styles. Among these cultural institutions, the MuCEM stands out as a prominent hub, delving into the historical and cultural heritage of Marseille and the broader Mediterranean region.

Marseille is a vibrant host to a diverse array of festivals that take place throughout the year. These include the Marseille Jazz des Cinq Continents festival, the Fiesta des Suds music festival, and the Marseille International Documentary Festival. These events draw in artists and performers from across the globe, creating a captivating cultural exchange within the city.

Music occupies a prominent role within the cultural tapestry of Marseille, encompassing a diverse range of genres and influences. The city boasts a wealth of musical heritage, spanning from traditional Provençal folk music to contemporary styles. Marseille has gained recognition for its dynamic hip-hop scene, which has birthed renowned artists like IAM and Fonky Family. Traditional Provençal music, characterized by its unique instruments and melodic patterns, is cherished and prominently featured during local festivals and cultural gatherings.

Culinary traditions form an integral part of Marseille's cultural fabric, representing the city's close proximity to the Mediterranean Sea and the abundant agricultural offerings of Provence. The local gastronomy showcases a delightful fusion of flavors and influences, incorporating fresh seafood, aromatic herbs like thyme and rosemary, the golden hues of olive oil, and the vibrant palette of seasonal vegetables. Bouillabaisse, a classic fish stew, holds an esteemed status as Marseille's quintessential dish and has garnered international acclaim. The city's bustling markets, such as the Marché de Noailles and the Vieux Port fish market, provide a feast for the senses, with vibrant showcases of fresh ingredients and the opportunity to indulge in local delicacies.

Sports, especially football (soccer), hold a profound significance within Marseille's cultural identity. Olympique de Marseille, one of the most accomplished football clubs in French history, calls the city its home. The passionate support and unwavering devotion of the Marseillais towards their team are palpable in the electrifying atmosphere that engulfs the Stade Vélodrome during matches. Football has emerged as a unifying element, fostering a sense of community and generating a powerful feeling of pride and belonging among the residents of Marseille.

Marseille's culture has been profoundly influenced by its multicultural populace, which has played a pivotal role in shaping the city's identity. Serving as a melting pot, Marseille has attracted individuals from various ethnic backgrounds, including those from North Africa, Italy, Armenia, and diverse corners of the world. These heterogeneous communities have enriched Marseille's cultural landscape, bringing with them their unique traditions, languages, and customs. The city actively celebrates its multiculturalism through a plethora of events, festivals, and communal gatherings that highlight the abundance and diversity of its residents, fostering a sense of unity and appreciation for different cultures.

Marseille's cultural calendar is replete with traditional festivals and events that hold a special place in the city's heritage. One such event is the Fête du Panier, which honors the historical Le Panier district. This celebration showcases a lively amalgamation of music, performances, and local customs, encapsulating the essence of Marseille's rich cultural fabric.

The Fête de la Saint-Victor commemorates the city's patron saint through processions, religious rituals, and a grand display of fireworks. Additionally, Marseille hosts the lively Carnaval de Marseille, a vibrant celebration featuring lively parades, flamboyant costumes, and captivating street performances. These festivities add a touch of vibrancy and excitement to Marseille's cultural landscape.

Marseille's architectural and historical legacy is evident in its landmarks and structures. The city proudly showcases a variety of notable sites, including the impressive Basilique Notre-Dame de la Garde, situated atop a hill and providing sweeping vistas of Marseille. The Vieux Port, the iconic old harbor, stands as a bustling focal point that has served as the heart of maritime activities for centuries. Marseille's architectural landscape is further enriched by remnants of ancient Greek and Roman influence, such as the Roman Docks and the Greek-inspired Corderie. These architectural gems offer glimpses into Marseille's rich past and contribute to its unique charm.

Urban Design and Neighborhoods

Located on the southeastern coastline of France, Marseille is positioned along the shores of the Mediterranean Sea. The city's urban fabric encompasses a harmonious blend of historical quarters, contemporary advancements, and breathtaking natural scenery.

The central focal point of Marseille is the Vieux Port, a historic harbor that has been a vital hub for the city since ancient times. This iconic district is teeming with liveliness, offering bustling markets, delectable seafood eateries, and picturesque waterfront promenades. From this vantage point, you can observe the constant ebb and flow of fishing vessels, yachts, and ferries that link Marseille to nearby islands and coastal destinations.

Situated north of the Vieux Port, the Le Panier neighborhood embodies Marseille's historical essence. Its labyrinthine, slender streets and vibrant facades paint a vivid picture of the city's past. Le Panier beckons visitors with its delightful assortment of quaint cafes, unique boutiques, and art galleries, providing an immersive experience into Marseille's rich heritage.

Continuing towards the east from the Vieux Port, you'll encounter the Joliette district, which has experienced noteworthy urban revitalization in recent times. This region boasts contemporary architectural gems, such as the remarkable MuCEM (Museum of European and Mediterranean Civilizations) and the bustling commercial hub of Les Terrasses du Port.

Further east, you will come across the residential areas of La Plaine and Cours Julien. These dynamic districts are celebrated for their bohemian ambiance, characterized by vibrant street art, fashionable boutiques, charming cafes, and a lively nightlife. Cours Julien, in particular, is famous for its bustling street markets and artistic expression.

Situated south of the Vieux Port is the Prado district, distinguished by its expansive boulevards, verdant parks, and stunning beaches. The Prado beaches, such as Plage du Prado and Plage Borély, provide ample opportunities for sunbathing, swimming, and engaging in various water sports.

Beyond the core of the city, Marseille expands into diverse districts and suburbs, each possessing its own distinct character and attractions.

NEIGHBORHOODS

Endoume, positioned in the southern section of Marseille, is an affluent residential district renowned for its exquisite architecture and breathtaking vistas of the Mediterranean Sea. The neighborhood boasts the enchanting Vallon des Auffes, a picturesque fishing harbor that adds to its charm.

Les Goudes, located on the periphery of Marseille, is a captivating fishing village characterized by its tranquil ambiance. The area presents magnificent coastal landscapes, rugged cliffs, and secluded beaches, attracting visitors seeking to engage in hiking, swimming, and immersing themselves in nature's beauty.

Saint-Victor, situated in close proximity to the Vieux Port, is renowned for its historical sites, which encompass the remarkable Basilique Notre-Dame de la Garde and the Fort Saint-Nicolas. The district possesses a captivating blend of narrow alleyways, ancient edifices, and lively squares, contributing to its overall charm.

Belsunce, in the heart of Marseille, is a vibrant and multicultural district. It is recognized for its lively street culture, diverse array of shops, and bustling markets like the Marché de Noailles, where a wide range of international products can be found.

La Canebière, Marseille's renowned boulevard, traverses the city center, pulsating with energy. This lively street is adorned with an array of shops, cafes, theaters, and historic structures. It stands as a vibrant epicenter for shopping and entertainment, attracting visitors and locals alike.

Les Catalans, close to the Prado beaches, is an enchanting residential district celebrated for its idyllic streets and delightful seaside villas. The neighborhood exudes a serene ambiance and offers captivating vistas of the Mediterranean Sea.

Saint-Barnabé, in the eastern region of Marseille, is renowned for its cozy village ambiance. The neighborhood boasts a delightful square, local shops, and a weekly market where visitors can explore an abundance of fresh produce and regional specialties.

La Valentine, on the eastern periphery of Marseille, is a suburban district recognized for its residential zones and commercial complexes. It offers a tranquil and predominantly residential environment, providing an escape from the bustling city center.

Les Aygalades, in the northern region of Marseille, is a culturally vibrant district with a notable North African influence. The neighborhood encompasses a blend of residential sections, markets, and local eateries that serve delectable ethnic cuisine.

Les Olives, in the western area of Marseille, is a residential district characterized by its serene and suburban atmosphere. The neighborhood is renowned for its olive groves and provides a peaceful retreat from the lively city center.

Belle de Mai, in the northeastern part of Marseille, is

a vibrant and multicultural neighborhood. It is recognized for its thriving artistic community, highlighted by spaces such as La Friche Belle de Mai. This former tobacco factory turned cultural center serves as a venue for exhibitions, performances, and workshops, contributing to the neighborhood's vibrant creative scene.

Les Chartreux, close to the city center, is an enchanting district celebrated for its narrow streets, vibrant houses, and quaint local shops. The neighborhood exudes a village-like atmosphere and is highlighted by the presence of Parc Longchamp, a stunning park featuring an impressive fountain and a natural history museum.

CHAPTER TWO

PLANNING YOUR TRIP TO MARSEILLE

Planning a trip to Marseille? Get ready for a captivating adventure in one of France's most dynamic cities. To make the most of your visit, careful planning is key. In this guide, we'll walk you through the essential steps, from choosing the right travel dates to booking accommodations and creating an itinerary that highlights the city's vibrant charm. So, get ready to immerse yourself in the sights, sounds, and flavors of Marseille as you plan an unforgettable journey.

Ideal Season to Visit

Marseille, a stunning city located along the southern shores of France, is a year-round destination that offers something special in every season. However, to optimize your visit, it's essential to carefully choose the ideal time to go. Marseille boasts a Mediterranean climate, featuring mild winters and hot summers.

Each season presents its own distinct allure and a variety of activities to enjoy. Let's explore the specifics to help you plan your trip to Marseille accordingly.

Winter (December to February):

In Marseille, winters are characterized by mild temperatures, typically ranging from 5°C (41°F) to 14°C (57°F). While it might not be the optimal season for beach-related activities, winter in Marseille possesses its own unique allure. The city adopts a tranquil ambiance, offering an opportunity to explore indoor attractions like museums and galleries without the usual crowds. Additionally, winter is an excellent time to savor Marseille's gastronomic delights, particularly indulging in hearty seafood dishes like bouillabaisse. If you visit in December, you can relish the festive spirit through Christmas markets and events.

Spring (March to May):

Marseille truly shines in the springtime, making it an ideal season to visit. The temperatures begin to rise, ranging from 10°C (50°F) to 20°C (68°F), creating a pleasant and comfortable atmosphere. The city bursts with vibrant blooms, and outdoor exploration becomes a joy. Take leisurely walks along the picturesque Old Port, delve into the historical wonders of the Le Panier neighborhood, or embark on a captivating boat tour to uncover the breathtaking beauty of the Calanques. Moreover, spring marks the commencement of various cultural events and festivals, such as the Marseille Jazz Festival and the Printemps de l'Art Contemporain (Contemporary Art Spring).

Summer (June to August):

Marseille's summer is synonymous with scorching temperatures, typically ranging from 25°C (77°F) to 30°C (86°F), making it the busiest time of the year for tourists. The city buzzes with excitement as visitors flock to embrace the sunny weather and vibrant beach culture. Relaxing under the sun at the Prado beaches, indulging in various water sports, or embarking on a journey to explore historical landmarks like the Notre-Dame de la Garde Basilica are all popular summer activities. It's important to note that summers can be crowded, resulting in longer queues and higher prices. To ensure a seamless experience, it's advisable to book accommodations and attractions in advance.

Autumn (September to November):

Marseille welcomes visitors with a delightful atmosphere during the autumn season. The temperatures gradually cool down, ranging from 15°C (59°F) to 25°C (77°F), providing a comfortable climate for outdoor activities. As the tourist crowds begin to dwindle, you can leisurely explore the city's attractions and landmarks at a more relaxed pace. Autumn also brings forth cultural events like the Fiesta des Suds, a lively music festival showcasing a variety of genres and celebrating world music. The city's parks and gardens come alive with vibrant foliage, offering picturesque scenery that will enchant nature enthusiasts.

In summary, the optimal time to visit Marseille varies based on individual preferences and desired experiences. Spring and autumn present favorable weather conditions, fewer crowds, and a flourishing cultural scene, making them well-suited for exploring the city. Summer caters to beach lovers and those seeking a vibrant atmosphere, while winter offers a more tranquil and reflective experience. When planning your trip to Marseille, consider your interests, budget, and preferred weather conditions to ensure a remarkable time in this captivating city.

Decide the Duration of Your Stay

Marseille has much to offer, so consider how many days you would like to spend exploring the city and its surroundings. A minimum of two to three days is recommended to fully appreciate the main attractions and soak in the local culture.

During your first day in Marseille, start by exploring

the vibrant Vieux Port (Old Port), the heart of the city. Stroll along the waterfront promenade and take in the picturesque views of fishing boats and yachts. Visit the historic Fort Saint-Jean, located at the entrance of the port, and explore its fascinating exhibits that showcase the city's maritime history. From there, venture into the winding streets of the Le Panier neighborhood, known for its colorful facades, charming cafes, and art galleries. Don't forget to visit the impressive Marseille Cathedral, a magnificent Roman Catholic basilica that offers panoramic views from its terrace.

On your second day, delve deeper into Marseille's cultural heritage. Explore the historic neighborhood of Le Cours Julien, known for its vibrant street art, bohemian atmosphere, and trendy boutiques. Visit the Musée des Civilisations de l'Europe et de la Méditerranée (MuCEM), a contemporary museum that focuses on Mediterranean civilizations and offers fascinating exhibitions. Take a leisurely stroll along the Corniche Kennedy, a scenic coastal road, and enjoy the stunning views of the Mediterranean Sea.

If you have an additional day or two, consider exploring the beautiful Calanques National Park, located just outside Marseille. These dramatic limestone cliffs, turquoise waters, and hidden coves offer a breathtaking natural landscape that is perfect for hiking, swimming, and sunbathing. Take a boat tour or hike to one of the many Calanques, such as Calanque de Sormiou or Calanque d'En-Vau, and immerse yourself in the pristine beauty of the Mediterranean coast.

Marseille is also known for its vibrant food scene, so be sure to sample the local cuisine during your stay. Indulge in bouillabaisse, a traditional fish stew, or enjoy fresh seafood at the local restaurants and markets. Don't miss the opportunity to explore the bustling Marché aux Poissons (Fish Market) and Marché de la Plaine (Produce Market) to experience the flavors and aromas of the region.

By allocating a minimum of two to three days for your stay in Marseille, you'll have sufficient time to explore the main attractions, soak in the local culture, and even venture into the stunning natural surroundings. However, if your schedule allows for a longer stay, you'll have the opportunity to delve deeper into Marseille's rich history, enjoy more outdoor activities, and truly immerse yourself in the vibrant atmosphere of this captivating city.

Visa requirements and necessary travel papers

Visa and travel document requirements differ based on your citizenship, the purpose, and length of your stay in a particular country. It is crucial to conduct thorough research and comprehend the precise visa prerequisites for your intended destination well ahead of your planned travel dates.

Visas are official papers issued by a country's government, which authorize individuals to enter, remain, or pass through that country for a designated duration. Certain countries have policies that exempt specific nationalities from requiring visas, enabling them to enter without a visa for a restricted period. However, for extended visits or specific purposes like employment or education, it may be mandatory to apply for a visa.

When seeking a visa, you typically need to complete an application form and furnish supporting materials such as a valid passport, passport-sized photos, evidence of your travel plans, proof of accommodation, financial records, and occasionally, an invitation letter or sponsorship. It is crucial to acknowledge that the visa application procedure may require significant time, hence it is recommended to initiate the process well ahead of your intended journey.

For a seamless and trouble-free travel experience, it is advisable to seek guidance from the embassy, consulate, or relevant immigration authorities of your intended destination country. This will enable you to acquire the most recent and precise details concerning visa prerequisites and travel documents.

To travel to Marseille, France, here is some general information about these requirements for visiting Marseille:

Schengen Visa:

Marseille is within the Schengen Area, a collection of 26 European countries that follow a unified visa policy. If you come from a country that is not exempt from the Schengen visa requirement, you will need to request a Schengen visa from the French embassy or consulate in your country of residence. This visa permits you to travel within the Schengen Area for a maximum duration of 90 days within a 180-day period.

Passport:

It is essential to have a passport that remains valid for at least six months after your intended departure from Marseille. It is advisable to have two empty pages in your passport to accommodate entry and exit stamps.

Entry Requirements for EU/EEA/Swiss Citizens:

Individuals who hold citizenship from a European Union (EU) member state, a country within the European Economic Area (EEA), or Switzerland can enter Marseille by presenting a valid national identity card or passport, without the requirement of a visa.

Visa-exempt Countries:

Nationals from specific countries, including the United States, Canada, Australia, New Zealand, Japan, South Korea, and several others, are permitted to enter Marseille and the Schengen Area for tourism or business activities without a visa. They can stay for a maximum of 90 days within a 180-day period under the visa-free or visa-waiver program. However, it is crucial to verify the specific visa requirements based on your nationality, as there might be additional conditions or limitations to consider.

It is important to emphasize that visa requirements are subject to change, making it advisable to regularly consult the official website of the French embassy or consulate in your country of residence, or the Ministry of Foreign Affairs website, for the latest and accurate information regarding visa requirements and necessary travel documents specific to your nationality.

Options for Transportation

Marseille, a lively port city situated in southern France, presents an array of transportation choices for travelers to traverse its delightful streets, historical sites, and stunning coastal regions. Whether you seek to discover the city's cultural highlights, explore its picturesque neighborhoods, or venture into the nearby surroundings, Marseille offers a diverse selection of transportation options tailored to meet the needs of every visitor. Below, we will explore the current transportation alternatives available to ensure that you can fully enjoy your time in Marseille.

Marseille City Pass:

To simplify your visit, the Marseille City Pass is a great option. This all-inclusive pass offers unrestricted use of the city's public transportation system, encompassing the metro, buses, and trams. Additionally, it provides complimentary admission to various attractions and museums, making it a budget-friendly choice for those interested in immersing themselves in Marseille's cultural richness.

Metro:

Marseille features a dependable and effective metro system, which comprises two lines: Line 1 (Blue Line) and Line 2 (Red Line). The metro provides connectivity to key areas of the city, offering a convenient means of transportation for covering longer distances efficiently. Operating from early morning until approximately midnight, the metro ensures frequent service, particularly during peak hours.

Bus:

Marseille's comprehensive bus network spans across the entire city, presenting visitors with convenient transportation choices. The extensive bus system enables access to destinations that may not be served by the metro and facilitates exploration of various neighborhoods. Typically operating from early morning until midnight, the buses also offer night services for those traveling during late hours.

Tramway:

Marseille's contemporary tramway system provides a reliable and pleasant means of transportation within the city. With three tram lines (T1, T2, and T3), it efficiently connects different neighborhoods and popular tourist destinations. Operating from early morning until late at night, the trams offer visitors a convenient and accessible mode of travel.

Bicycle Rental:

For a relaxed and immersive experience of Marseille's charm, renting a bicycle is highly recommended. The city's bike-sharing program, known as "Le vélo," offers a cost-effective and environmentally friendly means of exploring Marseille. You can rent bikes for short durations and enjoy leisurely rides along the city's dedicated bike lanes, particularly in coastal areas and parks. Moreover, several rental shops provide bicycles for longer periods, catering to those who wish to embark on extended explorations.

Walking:

Marseille's city center, with its charming neighborhoods, offers an ideal setting for walking enthusiasts. The compact nature of the city allows you to fully embrace its lively ambiance, uncover hidden treasures, and engage with the local culture firsthand. Whether you find yourself leisurely strolling along the historic Old Port, meandering through the vibrant Cours Julien district, or navigating the narrow alleyways of Le Panier, walking provides an intimate and immersive experience, enabling you to truly immerse yourself in Marseille's allure.

Taxi and Ride-Hailing Apps:

In Marseille, taxis are easily accessible, offering a convenient and comfortable means of transportation, especially for shorter trips or when carrying bulky luggage. Taxis can be hailed directly on the street or located at designated taxi stands across the city. Furthermore, ride-hailing apps such as Uber operate in Marseille, providing an alternative choice for visitors in need of immediate transportation services.

Boat Tours:

With its coastal setting and breathtaking seascapes, Marseille presents an enchanting opportunity for boat tours to discover the city and its environs. Numerous tour operators provide boat excursions that highlight Marseille's scenic coastline, Calanques National Park, and neighboring islands. These tours offer a distinct perspective, allowing you to appreciate the city's splendor from the sea.

Rental Cars and Scooters:

For those seeking independence and flexibility, Marseille offers various car rental companies. Renting a car allows you to go beyond the city limits and explore the picturesque Provence region at your leisure. Moreover, Marseille provides electric scooter rentals, offering a convenient choice for short trips within the city.

Conclusion:

Marseille offers a range of transportation options to accommodate the varied requirements of visitors, guaranteeing seamless and convenient travel within the city. Whether you choose the Marseille City Pass, public transportation, bicycles, walking, taxis, or boat tours, there is a mode of transportation that aligns with your preferences. By utilizing these current transportation choices, you can navigate Marseille effortlessly, uncover its fascinating history, immerse yourself in its lively culture, and create cherished memories of your experience in this captivating coastal city.

Check for Special Events

Checking for special events and festivals happening in Marseille during your visit is a great idea to enhance your experience and immerse yourself in the local culture. Here's more information on this:

Cultural Events, Marseille is known for its vibrant cultural scene, and there are numerous events taking place throughout the year. These can include music concerts, art exhibitions, theater performances, dance shows, and more. Keep an eye out for events organized at renowned venues like the Opéra de Marseille, the Silo, or the Docks des Suds. These events provide an opportunity to enjoy live performances and get a taste of the city's artistic atmosphere.

Festivals, Marseille hosts several festivals that showcase different aspects of its culture and heritage. One notable event is the Marseille Jazz des Cinq Continents, a renowned international jazz festival that brings together acclaimed artists from around the world. The Fête du Panier is another popular festival celebrated in the Le Panier neighborhood, featuring street performances, music, and local food. Additionally, there are film festivals, dance festivals, and even multicultural events that celebrate the diversity of Marseille's population. Checking the festival calendar can help you align your visit with these special events.

Local Events, Marseille has a vibrant local scene, and various neighborhood events take place throughout the year. These can include street markets, food fairs, neighborhood celebrations, and cultural exhibitions. These events provide a glimpse into the everyday life of the city and offer an opportunity to interact with locals and experience their traditions and customs.

To find out about special events and festivals happening during your visit, consider the following resources:

- Official Tourism Websites: Visit the official tourism websites of Marseille or the Provence region, as they often provide event calendars and information about upcoming festivals.

- Local Event Listings: Check local event listings in newspapers, online platforms, or community bulletin boards. These sources often highlight upcoming events in Marseille.

- Social Media and Online Communities: Join relevant online communities, social media groups, or forums related to Marseille. Locals or fellow travelers may share information about events and festivals happening in the city.

By keeping an eye on special events and festivals,

you can add unique experiences to your itinerary and make the most of your visit to Marseille.

CHAPTER THREE

TOP ATTRACTIONS IN MARSEILLE

Below are some of the must-see attractions in Marseille that you shouldn't overlook while exploring the city:

Vieux Port (Old Port):
Vieux Port, also known as the Old Port, stands as the vibrant focal point of Marseille. This historically significant waterfront area has served as the city's primary harbor since ancient times and continues to emanate a bustling and energetic ambiance. As you approach the Old Port, a picturesque sight unfolds before you, with colorful fishing boats gently swaying in the water.

The promenade that stretches alongside the harbor offers a delightful setting for a leisurely stroll, allowing you to immerse yourself in the maritime atmosphere. Here, you can observe the comings and goings of boats, witness local fishermen engrossed in their work, and perhaps even catch a glimpse of them selling their freshly caught seafood.

Vieux Port not only thrives as a hub for maritime activities but also presents itself as a culinary paradise. The area is dotted with charming cafes and restaurants where you can indulge in tantalizing seafood dishes. From the delicate flavors of freshly shucked oysters to the succulent delights of grilled fish and the rich complexity of savory bouillabaisse, the Old Port offers a diverse range of culinary experiences that beautifully showcase the gastronomic prowess of the region.

Throughout the year, the Old Port plays host to an array of events and festivals, injecting an additional dose of excitement into the area. Whether it's the traditional Provençal markets teeming with local produce and crafts or vibrant cultural festivals celebrating the city's heritage, there is always something happening at Vieux Port to captivate and entertain visitors.

With its charming waterfront location, lively atmosphere, and an abundance of delectable food options, the Old Port of Marseille holds an indispensable place on your itinerary. It captures the very essence of the city's maritime heritage and serves as an excellent introduction to the cultural and culinary wonders that Marseille has to offer.

Basilique Notre-Dame de la Garde:

Perched majestically atop a hill, Basilique Notre-Dame de la Garde proudly stands as one of Marseille's most renowned landmarks. This remarkable basilica presents an awe-inspiring sight, providing visitors with unparalleled panoramic vistas of the city, the captivating Mediterranean Sea, and the surrounding picturesque areas.

As you make your way up the hill towards the basilica, you'll be greeted by its impressive exterior, characterized by a captivating blend of Romanesque and Byzantine architectural styles. At the pinnacle of the basilica, the golden statue of the Virgin Mary, lovingly referred to as "La Bonne Mère," stands watch over Marseille, symbolizing protection for the city's seafarers.

Stepping inside Basilique Notre-Dame de la Garde, you'll be instantly captivated by the exquisite interior adorned with meticulously crafted mosaics, vibrant stained glass windows, and ornate embellishments. The level of craftsmanship and attention to detail is truly remarkable, creating an atmosphere of reverence and wonder.

Beyond its architectural grandeur, Basilique Notre-Dame de la Garde holds profound significance for the people of Marseille. It has long served as a place of devotion and pilgrimage, attracting both locals and visitors from far and wide. The basilica stands as a testament to Marseille's enduring maritime heritage, embodying faith, hope, and protection for the city and its seafaring community.

One of the highlights of a visit to Basilique Notre-Dame de la Garde is the opportunity to ascend the basilica's bell tower. Ascending the spiral staircase of the tower rewards you with breathtaking views that extend as far as the eye can see. From the bustling streets of Marseille to the glistening Mediterranean Sea, the vistas from the Basilique Notre-Dame de la Garde are truly awe-inspiring.

For its architectural magnificence and profound connection to Marseille's cultural and religious identity, a visit to Basilique Notre-Dame de la Garde is an essential part of any itinerary in the city. It offers not only the chance to marvel at the beauty of the basilica itself but also an opportunity to gain a fresh perspective on Marseille, admiring its expansive landscape from a vantage point that is both spiritually uplifting and awe-inspiring.

Calanques National Park:

Calanques National Park, located just a short distance from Marseille, is a remarkable natural treasure that guarantees an enthralling experience. This extraordinary park is characterized by its majestic cliffs made of limestone, the crystal-clear turquoise waters, and a landscape that beautifully showcases the allure of the Mediterranean coastline.

For outdoor enthusiasts and nature lovers, Calanques National Park is an idyllic haven. Its vast network of hiking trails meanders through the rugged terrain, offering awe-inspiring vistas of the dramatic cliffs, secluded coves, and pristine beaches. As you venture along these trails, you will find yourself immersed in a world of natural splendor, surrounded by the sights and sounds of untouched wilderness.

For a different perspective, boat tours provide an enchanting way to explore the wonders of the park. Cruising along the azure waters, you'll have the opportunity to marvel at the towering cliffs that majestically rise from the sea, leaving an indelible impression of their sheer magnificence. As the boat navigates through narrow passages and hidden inlets, you'll uncover secluded beaches and secret swimming spots, inviting you to bask in the tranquility of this coastal paradise.

The diversity of landscapes within Calanques National Park is truly astounding. From the rugged cliffs of Cap Canaille to the breathtaking fjord-like formations of Calanque de Sugiton, every corner of the park reveals a new and captivating vista. Whether you choose to hike, take a boat tour, or simply find a quiet spot to relax, Calanques National Park promises an unforgettable experience, surrounded by the grandeur of nature.

Preserving this exceptional natural site is of utmost importance, and visitors are encouraged to practice responsible tourism by respecting the park's guidelines and regulations. By doing so, you can contribute to the conservation efforts that ensure the future generations can continue to enjoy the pristine beauty of Calanques National Park.

A visit to Calanques National Park offers a unique opportunity to reconnect with nature, rejuvenate the soul, and marvel at the wonders of the natural world. Whether you decide to hike the trails, embark on a boat tour, or simply sit back and take in the breathtaking scenery, the park's awe-inspiring beauty will leave you with cherished memories that endure long after your visit has ended.

Château d'If:
Perched on the island of If, just a brief boat journey

from Marseille, the Château d'If commands attention as a renowned fortress steeped in captivating history. This iconic structure, formerly a prison, achieved worldwide recognition through Alexandre Dumas' literary masterpiece, "The Count of Monte Cristo." Exploring the Château d'If allows for a captivating journey through its storied past, panoramic vistas of the sea, and a chance to immerse oneself in the intrigue and drama that unfolded within its walls.

Upon setting foot on the island of If, the imposing presence of the Château d'If perched atop its rocky outcrop greets you. Initially constructed in the 16th century as a defensive stronghold, it later gained infamy as a prison during the 17th century. Its reputation as a formidable place of confinement became immortalized in literature through Dumas' famous novel.

Venturing inside the Château d'If transports you back in time, allowing you to tread the same corridors that once housed prisoners. The castle's walls whisper tales of intrigue, hardship, and resilience. Explore the various chambers and cells, and marvel at the remnants of the fortress's architecture, featuring arched ceilings, stone walls, and silent iron bars that bear witness to the castle's tumultuous history.

From the castle's ramparts, breathtaking panoramic

views of the Mediterranean Sea unfurl before your eyes. Take a moment to absorb the awe-inspiring scenery, where the azure waters meet the horizon, creating a captivating backdrop for this historic landmark. The tranquil surroundings contrast with the tales of confinement and secrecy that the fortress embodies.

A visit to the Château d'If also invites you to delve into the literary world of "The Count of Monte Cristo." As you explore the castle, you'll find yourself retracing the footsteps of the novel's protagonist, Edmond Dantès, and envisioning the struggles and triumphs that unfolded within these very walls. It's an opportunity to breathe life into Dumas' words and immerse yourself in the enthralling narrative that has captivated readers for generations.

The Château d'If stands as a testament to Marseille's rich history and serves as a reminder of the human stories that unfolded within its confines. It offers a unique blend of architectural grandeur, scenic beauty, and literary allure. A visit to this iconic fortress allows you to step back in time, connect with the past, and witness the enduring legacy of a place that continues to captivate the imagination of visitors from all corners of the world.

Les Terrasses du Port:

For those with a penchant for shopping and a fondness for modern architecture, Les Terrasses du Port is a must-visit destination. This contemporary shopping center presents a diverse selection of international and local brands, creating a haven for fashion enthusiasts and retail aficionados. However, Les Terrasses du Port offers more than just a shopping experience—it also boasts rooftop terraces that provide stunning panoramic views of the cityscape and the sparkling sea.

Upon entering Les Terrasses du Port, you'll be greeted by a sleek and stylish environment that harmoniously blends contemporary design with a vibrant atmosphere. The shopping center's open and spacious layout allows for a pleasant and comfortable shopping experience. As you explore the various levels and sections, you'll discover an array of renowned brands, boutiques, and specialty stores, offering an extensive range of fashion, accessories, beauty products, and more.

One of the highlights of Les Terrasses du Port lies in its rooftop terraces. Ascending to the top floors, you'll be rewarded with breathtaking views that stretch across Marseille and the glistening Mediterranean Sea. These expansive outdoor spaces provide the perfect setting to take a break from shopping, soak in the scenery, and capture memorable photos. Whether you choose to relax in a cozy lounge area or enjoy a meal at one of the rooftop restaurants, the panoramic vistas serve as a stunning backdrop, creating a unique and memorable experience.

Beyond its shopping and architectural allure, Les Terrasses du Port also hosts various events and activities throughout the year, adding an extra dimension of entertainment to your visit. From fashion shows and art exhibitions to live performances and seasonal celebrations, there's always something happening within the vibrant atmosphere of the shopping center.

Les Terrasses du Port caters to both fashion enthusiasts and those seeking a remarkable panoramic view of Marseille. It seamlessly blends the thrill of shopping with the pleasure of modern architecture and breathtaking vistas. Whether you're looking to update your wardrobe, relax and enjoy the views, or simply immerse yourself in the vibrant atmosphere, Les Terrasses du Port is a destination that offers an unforgettable experience for visitors of all tastes and preferences.

The Museums of Marseille

Marseille is renowned for its exceptional cultural scene, offering a multitude of exceptional museums that provide insights into its history, art, and heritage. Delve into the city's diverse cultural fabric through a visit to these distinctive museums, each offering a unique and enriching experience for visitors.

MuCEM (Museum of European and Mediterranean Civilizations):

Located at the entrance of the Vieux Port, the MuCEM (Museum of European and Mediterranean Civilizations) is a symbol of contemporary culture, offering a captivating journey into the diverse cultures that have influenced Europe and the Mediterranean. The museum's impressive architectural design seamlessly blends modern elements with traditional aesthetics, creating a striking visual presence that harmonizes with its surroundings.

Upon entering the MuCEM, visitors are immersed in a world of discovery and contemplation. Thoughtfully curated exhibitions explore the historical and contemporary aspects of European and Mediterranean civilizations, illuminating their shared heritage, influences, and interconnectedness. From ancient civilizations to present-day societies, the exhibitions provide a comprehensive understanding of the rich cultural tapestry that has flourished in these regions.

Inside the museum's galleries, multimedia

installations, interactive displays, and artistic interpretations come together to engage visitors in a multi-sensory exploration. Through a combination of artifacts, artworks, photographs, and audiovisual presentations, the MuCEM breathes life into history, traditions, and current issues, encouraging contemplation of the intricate complexities and diversity of European and Mediterranean cultures.

In addition to its permanent collections, the MuCEM hosts temporary exhibitions that delve into specific themes or showcase the works of renowned artists, further enriching the museum's dynamic nature. These exhibitions provide fresh perspectives, pushing boundaries and inviting visitors to engage with thought-provoking ideas and artistic expressions.

Beyond its exhibition spaces, the MuCEM serves as a vibrant cultural hub, hosting a variety of events such as lectures, workshops, film screenings, and performances. These gatherings foster dialogue, exchange, and deeper engagement with the themes explored in the museum, creating an interactive and lively cultural environment.

Furthermore, the MuCEM extends beyond its physical boundaries. Its strategic location at the entrance of the Vieux Port seamlessly integrates the museum with Marseille's urban landscape, connecting it to the city's maritime heritage and bustling atmosphere. The museum's outdoor areas, including its panoramic terrace, offer breathtaking views of the surrounding sea and cityscape, providing visitors with a unique perspective on Marseille's captivating beauty.

The MuCEM is evidence of Marseille's dedication to safeguarding its cultural legacy and promoting multicultural understanding. As visitors delve into the rich fabric of European and Mediterranean civilizations, a visit to this contemporary museum gives an opportunity for research, education, and inspiration. One can have a deeper appreciation for and knowledge of the complex cultural forces that define our global civilization by immersing oneself in the exhibitions.

Musée d'Histoire de Marseille (Marseille History Museum):

Nestled in the vibrant heart of Marseille, the Marseille History Museum invites visitors on an immersive journey through the city's rich and captivating past. This remarkable museum serves as a gateway to Marseille's history, showcasing archaeological treasures, fascinating artifacts, and interactive exhibits that span from ancient Greek and Roman eras to the present day. Moreover, the museum's location itself is steeped in historical significance, as it stands proudly on the very site of the ancient Greek port.

Stepping into the Marseille History Museum is like stepping back in time, as it unveils the layers of the city's captivating history. The museum's carefully curated collections bring the past to life, offering a glimpse into the lives, cultures, and events that have shaped Marseille over the centuries. From ancient artifacts and relics that illuminate the city's Greek and Roman roots to exhibits that delve into Marseille's maritime heritage and its role as a bustling Mediterranean port, the museum provides a comprehensive and immersive experience.

The Marseille History Museum boasts a diverse range of exhibits, each providing a window into a different chapter of the city's past. As visitors wander through the museum's halls, they can marvel at intricately crafted objects, intricate mosaics, and archaeological discoveries that have been meticulously preserved. The displays not only highlight the historical significance of Marseille but also shed light on the broader historical and cultural contexts in which the city evolved.

One of the museum's notable features is its interactive displays, which engage visitors of all ages in an educational and entertaining exploration of Marseille's history. Through multimedia presentations, immersive installations, and hands-on activities, visitors can actively participate in the learning process, gaining a deeper appreciation for the city's heritage.

The building itself is an architectural marvel, seamlessly blending the museum's contemporary design with the ancient foundations upon which it stands. The juxtaposition of the modern structure with the remnants of the ancient Greek port creates a captivating atmosphere that enhances the overall museum experience. Visitors can wander through the museum's different levels, marvel at the innovative design elements, and appreciate the careful integration of ancient and modern architectural styles.

Beyond its exhibits, the Marseille History Museum offers a range of educational programs, guided tours, and cultural events that further enrich the visitor's experience. These activities provide opportunities for deeper engagement, enabling visitors to delve into specific aspects of Marseille's history and interact with experts and scholars who share their knowledge and passion.

The dedication of the city to preserving and honoring its history is demonstrated by the presence of the Marseille History Museum. Both locals and visitors will find it to be a fascinating and educational experience as it immerses them in the intriguing history of Marseille. A trip to the Marseille History Museum will give you a deep understanding of the lasting heritage of this great city, regardless of whether you have a passion for history, archaeology, or are just curious about the city's origins.

MAC (Contemporary Art Museum):

The MAC (Contemporary Art Museum) in Marseille stands as a dynamic hub for modern and contemporary art, presenting a diverse range of artworks that push boundaries, challenge conventions, and provoke thought. This esteemed museum provides a platform for both established and emerging artists, offering visitors a captivating and ever-changing glimpse into the vibrant world of contemporary art.

Located in Marseille, a city renowned for its cultural vitality, the MAC embodies the spirit of artistic innovation and experimentation. Its expansive exhibition spaces provide a blank canvas for artists to showcase their creations across various mediums, including painting, sculpture, installation, photography, video, and performance art. The museum's commitment to showcasing a wide range of artistic expressions reflects the diverse and evolving nature of contemporary art.

At the MAC, visitors can expect a rotating roster of exhibitions that highlight the works of local, national, and international artists. From solo showcases to thematic group exhibitions, each presentation offers a unique perspective on contemporary art and invites viewers to engage with different artistic visions and narratives. The museum's curatorial team carefully selects and curates exhibitions that provoke thought, challenge preconceptions, and spark dialogue, creating a space for critical engagement and artistic exploration.

As visitors explore the MAC's galleries, they are immersed in a world of creativity and innovation. The artworks on display represent a multitude of perspectives, addressing a wide range of themes, from social and political issues to personal and philosophical inquiries. The museum encourages visitors to interpret and interact with the art, fostering a deeper connection and appreciation for contemporary artistic practices.

Beyond its exhibitions, the MAC also plays an active role in the cultural landscape of Marseille. The museum organizes a vibrant program of events and activities that complement its exhibitions, including artist talks, panel discussions, workshops, and performances. These events provide opportunities for visitors to engage directly with artists, curators, and art professionals, gaining insights into the creative process and expanding their understanding of contemporary art.

The MAC's commitment to education and community outreach is also evident through its initiatives aimed at fostering art appreciation among diverse audiences. The museum offers educational programs for students of all ages, guided tours, and workshops that promote artistic exploration and creativity. Through these initiatives, the MAC strives to make contemporary art accessible and engaging for everyone, nurturing a deeper appreciation for artistic expression and cultural diversity.

In conclusion, the MAC (Contemporary Art Museum) in Marseille stands as a vibrant and essential institution within the city's cultural landscape. With its ever-evolving exhibitions, commitment to artistic innovation, and engaging programs, the museum offers visitors an enriching and immersive experience in the world of contemporary art. Whether you are a seasoned art enthusiast or simply curious about the latest trends in artistic expression, a visit to the MAC promises to ignite your imagination and broaden your understanding of the dynamic realm of contemporary art.

Musée de la Moto et du Vélo (Motorcycle and Bicycle Museum):

The Musée de la Moto et du Vélo (Motorcycle and Bicycle Museum) is a haven for enthusiasts and aficionados of motorcycles and bicycles. Located in Marseille, this unique museum houses a captivating collection of vintage and rare two-wheeled vehicles, offering a comprehensive exploration of their history, design, and cultural significance.

As visitors step into the Musée de la Moto et du Vélo, they are transported into a world where the evolution of motorcycles and bicycles unfolds before their eyes. The museum showcases a wide variety of models, ranging from early prototypes and iconic classics to contemporary designs. Each exhibit tells a story, representing a particular era or highlighting a significant technological advancement in the realm of two-wheeled transportation.

The museum's collection spans different styles and genres, reflecting the diversity of motorcycles and bicycles throughout history. From sleek and powerful racing motorcycles to elegant and functional city bicycles, the exhibits demonstrate the ingenuity of engineers, the artistry of designers, and the craftsmanship of manufacturers.

One of the highlights of the Musée de la Moto et du

Vélo is the opportunity to observe the intricate details and unique features of these vehicles up close. Visitors can appreciate the fine craftsmanship, the evolution of engineering techniques, and the innovative design elements that have shaped the development of motorcycles and bicycles over time. The museum provides a glimpse into the past, allowing visitors to connect with the nostalgia and the timeless allure of these beloved modes of transport.

In addition to the physical exhibits, the Musée de la Moto et du Vélo also offers informative displays, interactive presentations, and multimedia installations that enhance the visitor experience. These educational resources provide insights into the historical and cultural contexts surrounding motorcycles and bicycles, exploring their impact on society, mobility, and popular culture.

For enthusiasts, the Musée de la Moto et du Vélo is a treasure trove of knowledge and inspiration. It offers a unique opportunity to delve into the world of vintage and rare two-wheeled vehicles, to appreciate their aesthetics, and to understand the technological advancements that have shaped their evolution. Whether you are a passionate collector, an admirer of mechanical engineering, or simply curious about the history of motorcycles and bicycles, a visit to this museum promises an immersive and enriching experience.

The Musée de la Moto et du Vélo is a tribute to the bikes and motorcycles' ongoing appeal and cultural importance. The museum maintains and commemorates the heritage of these legendary cars through its sizable collection and interesting displays, paying honor to their legacy and encouraging future generations to appreciate their beauty and historical significance.

Neighborhood Markets in Marseille

Vieux Port Market
This lively market is situated close to the Old Port and presents a charming selection of recently harvested goods, distinctive local dishes, and artisanal crafts. Take the opportunity to wander through the vibrant stalls adorned with a variety of vivid fruits, vegetables, cheeses, spices, and other mouthwatering delicacies. It's an exceptional destination to immerse yourself in the tastes of Provence and engage with the friendly merchants.

Marché de la Plaine
The Cours Julien neighborhood springs to life on Tuesdays, Thursdays, and Saturdays with the vibrant Marché de la Plaine. This well-liked market provides

a diverse range of farm-fresh fruits and vegetables, clothing, antiques, books, and vintage collectibles. It's a fantastic spot to leisurely explore, discover one-of-a-kind gems, and soak up the authentic local ambiance.

Marché des Capucins

The bustling and multiracial Marché des Capucins is located in the Noailles district. A wide variety of international fruits, vegetables, spices, meats, and seafood are available here. The market also sells goods from North Africa and the Middle East, showcasing the multiculturalism of Marseille.

Marché du Prado

This sizable outdoor market, which lies on the Prado Boulevard, provides a huge variety of fresh foods, flowers, cheese, and other regional goods. Both locals and tourists are drawn to the market by its high-quality ingredients and vibrant atmosphere.

Local Cuisine

Exploring the local cuisine is a must when visiting Marseille. The city is renowned for its delicious food, particularly its seafood dishes. Here's more information on the local cuisine and where to experience it:

Bouillabaisse is a traditional fish stew that originated in Marseille. It is made with a variety of fish and seafood, cooked in a flavorful broth of tomatoes, herbs, and spices. This iconic dish is best enjoyed at one of the many seafood restaurants in Marseille, where it is often prepared according to time-honored recipes. Some popular places to try bouillabaisse include Chez Fonfon, Miramar, and L'Epuisette.

Socca is a popular street food in Marseille. It is a thin, savory pancake made from chickpea flour, olive oil, and seasoned with salt and pepper. You can find socca being cooked on large griddles in markets and street stalls. La Pignata, located in the Noailles neighborhood, is a popular spot to savor this local specialty.

To truly experience the vibrant food culture of Marseille, visit the local markets. The Vieux-Port Fish Market is a bustling hub where you can find a wide variety of fresh seafood, including fish, shellfish, and crustaceans. Noailles Market, located in the multicultural Noailles district, is known for its diverse range of fruits, vegetables, spices, and international food products. Exploring these markets allows you to immerse yourself in the vibrant atmosphere and discover local ingredients.

Marseille offers a delightful array of street food options. You can try panisses, which are deep-fried chickpea fritters, or navettes, boat-shaped orange blossom-scented cookies, both of which are popular snacks in the city. Street food vendors and food trucks can be found in various areas, offering a wide range of delicious treats to satisfy your cravings.

Marseille is home to numerous restaurants that showcase the city's culinary delights. From traditional Provençal cuisine to innovative fusion dishes, you'll find a wide range of options to suit your taste. Le Petit Nice Passedat, Le Café des Epices, and La Boîte à Sardine are a few notable restaurants that offer exceptional dining experiences.

When exploring the local cuisine, don't forget to pair your meals with local wines, such as the famous rosé wines from the Provence region.

By diving into the local food scene, you can indulge in the flavors of Marseille and experience the culinary traditions that make the city unique.

Exploring the Outdoors in and Near Marseille

Sailing and Boating

Sailing and boating opportunities abound in Marseille, thanks to its picturesque coastal setting. The city offers an exceptional experience for those seeking maritime adventures. Whether you're an experienced sailor or a novice enthusiast, there are various options available to cater to your interests.

Renting a sailboat, motorboat, or catamaran allows you to embark on exciting journeys and explore the vast expanse of the Mediterranean Sea. As you navigate the crystal-clear waters, you can soak in the breathtaking coastal scenery, feel the refreshing sea breeze on your face, and revel in the freedom that sailing offers.

For a leisurely outing, you can opt for a relaxing cruise, allowing you to unwind and appreciate the beauty of Marseille's coastline. Sunbathe on the deck, admire the stunning views, and let the gentle waves lull you into a state of tranquility.

If you're an avid angler, fishing excursions are available, giving you the chance to cast your line and try your luck at catching some local marine species. Engaging in this age-old pastime amidst the serene waters can be both thrilling and rewarding.

For those looking to learn the ropes of sailing, Marseille provides an excellent opportunity to enroll in sailing lessons. Professional instructors will guide you through the basics, teaching you essential skills and techniques to navigate the waters with confidence. Whether you aspire to become a seasoned sailor or simply want to gain a new hobby, these lessons offer an immersive and educational experience.

Scuba Diving

Scuba diving enthusiasts will find themselves captivated by the exceptional diving opportunities that Marseille has to offer. The city boasts a vibrant underwater ecosystem, teeming with diverse marine life and fascinating underwater landscapes.

Embarking on a scuba diving adventure in Marseille allows you to delve into the depths of the Mediterranean Sea and witness the beauty that lies beneath its surface. Immerse yourself in an enchanting world of colorful corals, graceful sea creatures, and unique underwater plant species. From schools of shimmering fish to mesmerizing sea turtles, you'll have the chance to encounter a plethora of marine life up close and personal.

One of the highlights of diving in Marseille is the opportunity to explore historical shipwrecks that have become havens for marine organisms. These submerged relics provide an intriguing glimpse into the region's maritime history while offering a thrilling diving experience. Swim amidst the remnants of sunken vessels, witnessing the convergence of nature and history in a truly awe-inspiring manner.

Diving centers in Marseille cater to both beginners

and experienced divers, ensuring that everyone can partake in this exhilarating activity. Whether you're new to scuba diving or a seasoned professional, these centers provide the necessary equipment and guidance for safe and enjoyable underwater exploration. Expert instructors are available to accompany and assist divers, offering valuable insights into the marine environment and ensuring a memorable and secure diving experience.

Rock climbing

Rock climbing enthusiasts will find themselves in paradise when exploring Marseille and its surrounding areas. With its diverse terrain and stunning cliffs, the region offers a plethora of rock climbing opportunities suitable for climbers of all levels.

One of the most popular rock climbing destinations in Marseille is the Calanques. These picturesque limestone cliffs rise majestically from the turquoise waters of the Mediterranean Sea, providing a breathtaking backdrop for climbers. The Calanques offer a range of routes catering to different skill levels, from beginner-friendly ascents to more challenging vertical challenges. As you conquer the cliffs, you'll be rewarded with awe-inspiring views of the coastline and the sparkling sea below.

In addition to the Calanques, nearby areas such as Les Goudes and Sainte-Victoire are also renowned for their excellent rock climbing spots. Les Goudes, located just outside Marseille, features rugged cliffs and rugged landscapes that provide thrilling climbing experiences. Sainte-Victoire, located a short distance from Marseille, offers a unique setting with its distinctive mountain formation and a variety of climbing routes to suit all abilities.

When venturing into the world of rock climbing in Marseille, it is highly advisable to climb with a guide or experienced climbers who are familiar with the routes and safety precautions. They can provide valuable guidance, ensure proper equipment usage, and enhance your overall climbing experience while prioritizing safety.

Marseille's rock climbing scene not only offers an adrenaline-pumping adventure but also allows climbers to connect with nature and enjoy the serenity of their surroundings. Scaling the cliffs, testing your limits, and experiencing the exhilaration of reaching new heights create a profound sense of accomplishment and a deep appreciation for the natural beauty of the region.

Whether you're a seasoned climber or a beginner looking to embark on your first climbing expedition,

Marseille and its surroundings provide an array of rock climbing opportunities that will satisfy your adventurous spirit. Strap on your harness, grab your climbing shoes, and get ready to conquer the vertical challenges that await you in this breathtaking landscape.

Paragliding

For those in search of an exhilarating adventure, paragliding over Marseille offers a unique and breathtaking experience. This thrilling activity allows you to soar through the skies, feeling the rush of wind against your face while being treated to awe-inspiring views of the city, coastline, and surrounding landscapes.

Paragliding in Marseille provides the opportunity to witness the region's beauty from a completely different perspective. As you launch into the air, you'll be greeted by panoramic vistas that stretch as far as the eye can see. Marvel at the azure waters of the Mediterranean, the sprawling cityscape dotted with historical landmarks, and the picturesque natural landscapes that surround Marseille.

Even if you have no prior paragliding experience, tandem flights are available, allowing you to enjoy this exhilarating activity with the guidance of an experienced pilot. Strap yourself into the secure harness, and let the professional take care of the technical aspects while you sit back, relax, and soak in the awe-inspiring views. Tandem flights are not only safe but also provide an excellent opportunity for beginners to experience the thrill of paragliding without the need for extensive training.

As you glide through the air, suspended beneath a colorful canopy, you'll feel a sense of freedom and liberation. The unique combination of adrenaline and serenity makes paragliding a truly unforgettable experience. Capture breathtaking photos, make memories that will last a lifetime, and gain a newfound appreciation for the beauty of Marseille and its surroundings.

Whether you're an adrenaline junkie seeking an unforgettable rush or simply a curious traveler wanting to explore the region from a different perspective, this activity promises an unparalleled experience. Soar high above the landscape, embrace the freedom of the skies, and create memories that will stay with you forever.

CHAPTER FOUR

MARSEILLE LANGUAGE AND ETIQUETTE NAVIGATION

To explore Marseille and communicate with the locals, it's helpful to have some familiarity with the language and etiquette of the region. Here are some essential features of the language and manners in Marseille:

Language

French

In Marseille, the official language spoken is French. While English is often understood and spoken in tourist areas and establishments, it is generally appreciated when visitors make an effort to greet locals and interact using basic French phrases. Simple greetings such as "Bonjour" (Hello), "Merci" (Thank you), and "S'il vous plaît" (Please) can go a long way in showing respect for the local culture and establishing a friendly connection with the residents.

Even if your French skills are limited, attempting to use these phrases demonstrates goodwill and can enhance your overall experience in Marseille. Additionally, it's always helpful to carry a pocket-sized phrasebook or have a translation app handy to assist in communication if needed.

Local Accent

One notable aspect of Marseille's cultural identity is its distinct regional accent and dialect known as "Marseillais." This local accent sets Marseille apart from other French-speaking regions and can be quite distinct from standard French. The Marseillais accent is characterized by unique pronunciations, intonations, and vocabulary that may initially sound unfamiliar to those accustomed to traditional French.

While it can be challenging for visitors to fully comprehend the Marseillais accent, making an effort to understand and embrace it is highly appreciated by the locals. Showing an interest in the local dialect demonstrates a genuine respect for Marseille's cultural heritage and can help forge connections with the community. Even if you find it difficult to replicate the accent, listening attentively and being open-minded towards the linguistic differences can go a long way in fostering positive interactions with the people of Marseille.

Engaging in conversations with locals and asking them to clarify or repeat certain phrases can provide an opportunity to learn more about the Marseillais accent and deepen your understanding of the local culture. The residents of Marseille are generally proud of their accent and appreciate visitors who show an interest in their unique linguistic traditions. Embracing the Marseillais accent, even in small ways, can enhance your experience in Marseille and create memorable interactions with the locals.

Etiquette

Greetings

When meeting someone for the first time or entering a shop or restaurant, it's customary to greet people with a friendly "Bonjour" (Hello) or "Bonsoir" (Good evening). Handshakes are the typical form of greeting, although close friends and family may exchange kisses on the cheeks.

Politeness

Politeness is highly valued in Marseille. It's important to say "S'il vous plaît" (Please) and "Merci" (Thank you) when interacting with locals. Addressing people with "Monsieur" (Sir) or "Madame" (Madam) shows respect.

Dining Etiquette

When dining in Marseille, it's customary to wait for the host to invite you to sit at the table. Keep your hands on the table, but not your elbows. Remember to say "Bon appétit" (Enjoy your meal) before you start eating. It's also polite to finish everything on your plate as wasting food is considered disrespectful.

Dress Code

Marseille has a relaxed and casual atmosphere, but it's still advisable to dress appropriately when visiting churches, museums, or upscale establishments. Avoid wearing beachwear or overly revealing clothing in public places.

Tipping

In Marseille, tipping is not obligatory, but it's appreciated for good service. A general rule of thumb is to leave a small tip, usually rounding up the bill or leaving a 5-10% tip in restaurants.

Personal Space

Marseille is known for its warm and friendly people, but it's important to respect personal space. Maintain an appropriate distance when interacting with others and avoid touching or hugging someone unless you have developed a close relationship.

Time Management

It is advisable to be on time for meetings, appointments, and reservations because Marseille values timeliness. Social events, however, could take a lazier attitude to punctuality.

Basic French Phrases and Pronunciation Guide

Here are some basic French phrases along with their pronunciation guide:

1. Hello: Bonjour (bohn-zhoor)
2. Goodbye: Au revoir (oh ruh-vwahr)
3. Please: S'il vous plaît (seel voo pleh)
4. Thank you: Merci (mehr-see)
5. You're welcome: De rien (duh ryehn)
6. Yes: Oui (wee)
7. No: Non (nohn)
8. Excuse me: Excusez-moi (ehk-skoo-zay mwa)
9. I'm sorry: Je suis désolé(e) (zhuh swee day-zoh-lay)
10. Do you speak English?: Parlez-vous anglais ? (par-lay voo ahn-glay)
11. I don't understand: Je ne comprends pas (zhuh nuh kohm-prahn pah)
12. Can you help me?: Pouvez-vous m'aider ? (poo-vez voo may-day)
13. How much does it cost?: Combien ça coûte ?

(kohm-byehn sah koot)

Please note that French pronunciation can be tricky, but here are some general guidelines to help you:

- The French "r" sound is a soft, guttural sound produced at the back of the throat.
- Pay attention to nasal sounds, indicated by the letter combinations "an," "en," "in," "on," and "un." They are pronounced with a nasalized vowel sound.
- "J" is pronounced like the "s" in "measure," while "g" is pronounced like the "s" in "pleasure" when followed by "e," "i," or "y."
- "U" is pronounced like the "oo" in "too."
- Silent letters are common in French, so pay attention to the sounds of the surrounding letters.

Remember, practice makes perfect when it comes to pronunciation. Listening to native speakers, using language learning resources, and practicing with a language partner can help you improve your pronunciation and fluency in French.

Basic Marseillais Phrases and Pronunciation Guide

Marseillais is a regional accent and dialect of the French language spoken in Marseille. It has its unique characteristics and pronunciation. Here are some basic Marseillais phrases along with their pronunciation guide:

1. Hello: Salut (sah-loo)
2. How are you?: Ça va ? (sah vah)
3. What's up?: Quoi de neuf ? (kwah duh nuhf)
4. Thank you: Mercé (mehr-say)
5. You're welcome: De rin (duh ran)
6. Yes: Ouais (waa)
7. No: Nen (neh)
8. Excuse me: Escusa-moi (ess-koo-sah mwa)
9. I'm sorry: Suis désolé(e) (swee day-zoh-lay)
10. Do you speak English?: Tu parles anglais ? (too parl ahn-glay)
11. I don't understand: Comprends pas (kohm-prahn pah)
12. Can you help me?: Tu peux m'aider ? (too puhz may-day)
13. How much does it cost?: Ça coûte combien ? (sah koot kohm-byehn)
14. Where is...?: Il est où... ? (eel ay oo)
15. I would like...: Vourrè... (voo-ray)

Please note that Marseillais pronunciation can vary, and it has its distinct sounds and intonations. The best way to grasp the Marseillais accent and dialect is to listen to native speakers and immerse yourself in the local culture. Practicing with locals or language exchange partners from Marseille can also help you get a better understanding of the specific nuances of Marseillais pronunciation.

Keep in mind that Marseillais is not a separate language but a regional variation of French, so the standard French phrases shared earlier can also be understood and used in Marseille.

Dos and Don'ts of the Cultural Behavior in Marseille

When visiting Marseille, it's essential to be mindful of the local culture and customs. Here are some cultural do's and don'ts to help you navigate Marseille with respect:

Do's:
- Engage in friendly conversations with locals. Marseille is known for its friendly and outgoing people, so don't hesitate to strike up a conversation and learn more about their way of life.

- Embrace the local cuisine and try traditional dishes like bouillabaisse (fish stew), socca (chickpea pancake), and pastis (anise-flavored liqueur).

- Explore the local markets and engage in friendly conversations with vendors. Bargaining is not common in Marseille, but polite negotiation may be accepted in certain situations.

- Appreciate the local arts and culture by visiting museums, galleries, and attending cultural events such as music festivals, theater performances, or traditional dance shows.

- Be open to trying new things. Marseille is a city of culinary delights, so don't be afraid to sample local dishes, explore street food, and indulge in the flavors of Provence.

- Respect the local customs and traditions. Marseille has a rich cultural heritage, and it's important to be mindful of local customs and practices. For example, in religious sites, observe any rules or guidelines specific to that place.

- Enjoy the local outdoor activities and take advantage of Marseille's beautiful coastline. Go for a swim, relax on the beaches, or take a boat trip to the nearby Calanques, stunning limestone cliffs and coves along the Mediterranean coast.

- Embrace the café culture. Take the time to sit at a café terrace, sip a coffee, and people-watch. It's a popular pastime in Marseille and a great way to immerse yourself in the local lifestyle.

- Respect the environment. Marseille is surrounded by natural beauty, including the Calanques National Park. When exploring the outdoors, follow designated trails, avoid littering, and leave the environment as you found it.

Don'ts:

- Don't assume that everyone speaks English. While many people in tourist areas may speak English, it's always polite to ask if someone can communicate in English before assuming.

- Avoid discussing sensitive topics like politics or religion, as these can be divisive and best approached with caution.

- Don't rush through meals. In Marseille, dining is a leisurely affair, so take your time to savor the food and enjoy the company.

- Refrain from making negative generalizations or stereotypes about Marseille or its residents. Every city has its unique characteristics, and it's important to approach it with an open mind.

- Avoid making loud or disruptive noise in public places. Marseille, like any other city, appreciates a peaceful environment, so be mindful of your noise level, especially in residential areas or public transportation.

- Avoid excessive displays of wealth or flashy attire, as it may attract unwanted attention. Blend in with the locals and dress modestly, especially in more traditional or residential areas.

- Don't forget to carry some cash with you. While credit cards are widely accepted, smaller establishments and local markets may prefer cash transactions.

- Avoid excessive public displays of affection. While holding hands or a quick kiss is generally acceptable, more intimate displays of affection may be best kept in private.

- Avoid drinking excessively in public areas. While enjoying a glass of wine or a beer at a restaurant or café is common, public drunkenness is generally frowned upon.

By being respectful, open-minded, and embracing the local culture, you'll have a more authentic and memorable experience during your visit in Marseille.

CHAPTER FIVE

TOURIST LODGING OPTIONS IN MARSEILLE

Marseille offers a wide range of accommodation options to suit different budgets and preferences. From luxury hotels to budget-friendly hostels and vacation rentals, here are some recommendations for accommodation in Marseille:

Luxury Hotels

One notable luxury hotel in Marseille is the Hotel Sofitel Marseille Vieux-Port. Situated in a prime location overlooking the picturesque Old Port, this five -star establishment exudes elegance and style. The hotel boasts spacious and beautifully appointed rooms, featuring modern decor, plush furnishings, and stunning views of the harbor or city. Guests can indulge in a range of amenities, including a rooftop pool, a wellness center, exquisite dining options, and impeccable concierge services.

Another renowned option is the InterContinental Marseille - Hotel Dieu. Housed in a historic building that was once a hospital, this five-star hotel seamlessly blends contemporary luxury with architectural grandeur. The elegantly designed rooms offer a perfect combination of comfort and sophistication, and the hotel features a spa, fitness center, and an array of dining options that showcase the region's culinary delights.

The Radisson Blu Hotel, Marseille Vieux Port, is yet another top choice for luxury accommodations in the city. Located near the Old Port, this upscale hotel offers stylish rooms with modern amenities, providing a serene and comfortable retreat for guests. The hotel features a rooftop terrace with panoramic views, a wellness center, a gourmet restaurant, and exceptional service to ensure a truly indulgent experience.

These luxury hotels in Marseille go above and beyond to provide a seamless blend of opulence, comfort, and personalized service. From the moment you step into their elegant lobbies, you'll be greeted by attentive staff who strive to exceed your expectations and cater to your every need.

Whether you're visiting Marseille for business or leisure, these luxury hotels offer a sanctuary of refinement where you can relax, rejuvenate, and indulge in the city's charms. Immerse yourself in the lap of luxury, revel in the world-class amenities, and savor the impeccable service that epitomizes the hospitality of Marseille's finest establishments.

Boutique Hotels

Hotel C2 stands out as one of Marseille's most prestigious boutique hotels. Housed in a stunning 19th-century mansion, this refined establishment seamlessly blends historic charm with contemporary design. Each room is individually decorated with luxurious furnishings, unique artwork, and modern amenities. Hotel C2 also features a rooftop terrace with panoramic views, a spa, and a gourmet restaurant, creating an oasis of elegance and tranquility.

Le Petit Nice Passedat, a renowned three-Michelin-starred restaurant, also offers an exquisite boutique hotel experience. Situated on the waterfront, this family-owned establishment combines Mediterranean charm with exceptional service. The hotel's rooms exude elegance and sophistication, with tasteful decor, sea views, and luxurious amenities. Guests can savor the culinary delights of Chef Gérald Passedat's renowned seafood cuisine, indulge in spa treatments, and bask in the beauty of the Mediterranean just steps away.

Mama Shelter Marseille presents a vibrant and contemporary boutique hotel experience. Located in the heart of the city, this trendy hotel features stylish and eclectic rooms that reflect the creative spirit of Marseille. With vibrant colors, quirky design elements, and modern amenities, Mama Shelter Marseille offers a hip and energetic atmosphere. Guests can enjoy the hotel's rooftop terrace, lively restaurant and bar, and a range of amenities designed to create a fun and memorable stay.

These boutique hotels in Marseille pride themselves on providing a personalized and intimate experience, focusing on the details that make each guest feel truly special. From unique decor and curated artwork to attentive and friendly staff, these establishments aim to create a warm and inviting ambiance that reflects the city's charm.

Mid-Range Hotels

Marseille offers a variety of mid-range hotels that strike a balance between affordability and comfort, ensuring a pleasant stay without compromising on convenience or quality. These establishments provide comfortable rooms, essential amenities, and a central location, making them ideal choices for travelers seeking value for their money.

Hotel La Residence du Vieux Port is a highly regarded mid-range option in Marseille. Located on the iconic Old Port, this hotel offers well-appointed rooms with modern decor and panoramic views of the harbor. Guests can enjoy a range of amenities, including a rooftop terrace, a bar, and attentive service, all within a short distance from popular attractions and dining options.

Hotel Novotel Marseille Vieux Port is another popular mid-range choice. Situated in the bustling Vieux Port neighborhood, this hotel provides contemporary rooms equipped with comfortable furnishings and modern amenities. The hotel features a rooftop pool, a fitness center, a restaurant, and a welcoming atmosphere that caters to both business and leisure travelers.

Hotel Escale Oceania Marseille Vieux Port offers affordable yet comfortable accommodation near the Old Port. The hotel's rooms are tastefully decorated, featuring essential amenities for a pleasant stay. Guests can take advantage of the hotel's breakfast buffet, a cozy lounge area, and a convenient location within walking distance of popular landmarks and transportation hubs.

These mid-range hotels in Marseille prioritize affordability while ensuring a comfortable and enjoyable stay. They serve as excellent bases for exploring the city's attractions, dining at local restaurants, and immersing oneself in the vibrant atmosphere of Marseille.

With their central locations and essential amenities, these mid-range hotels offer a convenient and affordable option for travelers looking to make the most of their stay in Marseille.

Budget-Friendly Hotels
Marseille caters to budget-conscious travelers with a selection of budget-friendly hotels that provide affordable rates without compromising on quality or comfort. These establishments offer a range of amenities and convenient locations, ensuring a pleasant stay while keeping costs in check.

Hotel ibis Marseille Centre Gare Saint Charles is a

popular budget-friendly choice. Located near the city's main train station, this hotel offers functional and comfortable rooms at affordable prices. Guests can enjoy amenities such as free Wi-Fi, a bar, and a 24-hour reception, making it a convenient option for travelers arriving by train or seeking easy access to public transportation.

Another budget-friendly option is Hotel ibis Budget Marseille Vieux Port. Situated near the Old Port, this hotel offers compact yet well-designed rooms with essential amenities. The hotel's reasonable rates make it an attractive choice for budget travelers who still want to experience the city's vibrant atmosphere and explore popular attractions within walking distance.

Hotel Première Classe Marseille Centre is a budget-friendly hotel known for its affordability and convenience. Located in the city center, it offers compact rooms equipped with necessary amenities such as air conditioning, free Wi-Fi, and en-suite bathrooms. The hotel's prime location provides easy access to Marseille's sights, shopping districts, and dining options, allowing budget travelers to make the most of their stay.

These budget-friendly hotels in Marseille understand the importance of providing comfortable accommodations at affordable prices. They aim to meet the needs of budget-conscious travelers who seek value for their money without sacrificing convenience or quality.

By choosing these budget-friendly options, travelers can allocate their resources to exploring Marseille's attractions, trying local cuisine, and immersing themselves in the city's vibrant culture, all while enjoying a comfortable and budget-conscious stay.

Whether you're a backpacker, a budget traveler, or simply looking for affordable accommodations, these budget-friendly hotels in Marseille offer a practical and economical choice without compromising on essential amenities or a convenient location.

Vacation Rentals
If you're seeking a more independent and home-like experience during your stay in Marseille, booking a vacation rental is an excellent option. Vacation rentals provide the opportunity to immerse yourself in the local culture, enjoy extra space and privacy, and have the freedom to create your own schedule.

Websites such as Airbnb, HomeAway, and Booking.com offer a wide range of vacation rentals in Marseille, including apartments and houses suited for short-term stays. These platforms allow you to browse through numerous listings, filter by your preferences, and find the perfect accommodation to suit your needs.

Opting for a vacation rental in Marseille offers several advantages. Firstly, you'll have access to a variety of property types and sizes, ranging from cozy studios to spacious houses, allowing you to choose the option that best accommodates your group size and preferences. Many rentals are equipped with amenities such as kitchens, living areas, and laundry facilities, providing you with the comforts and conveniences of a home away from home.

Additionally, vacation rentals often offer a more personalized experience. Hosts are typically locals who can provide valuable insights and recommendations about the city, including hidden gems, local attractions, and dining options. This local perspective can enhance your overall experience and help you discover the authentic side of Marseille.

Booking a vacation rental also allows you to live like a local. You can shop at neighborhood markets, prepare your own meals, and experience the rhythm of daily life in Marseille. This level of immersion provides a deeper connection to the city and its culture, making your stay more meaningful and memorable.

However, it's important to carefully review the details of each vacation rental listing, including guest reviews, amenities, and cancellation policies. Take note of the location, proximity to public transportation, and any additional fees or requirements. By doing so, you can ensure that the vacation rental you choose aligns with your preferences and expectations.

Hostels

For backpackers and budget-conscious travelers visiting Marseille, the city offers a range of hostels that provide affordable accommodation options and a vibrant social atmosphere. These hostels cater to those looking to meet fellow travelers, enjoy communal facilities, and keep costs low while exploring the city.

Hostel Vertigo Vieux-Port is a popular choice among backpackers. Located near the Old Port, this hostel offers dormitory-style rooms with shared bathrooms and communal areas. The lively atmosphere and friendly staff create a welcoming environment for guests to socialize and connect with other travelers. With its central location, Hostel Vertigo Vieux-Port provides easy access to Marseille's attractions, nightlife, and public transportation.

Hostel Mama Shelter Marseille is another well-known option that combines affordability with style. Situated in the city center, this trendy hostel features modern and colorful rooms, a communal kitchen, and a lively bar area. The hostel's energetic atmosphere, comfortable common spaces, and regular events make it a great choice for backpackers looking for a social experience.

Vertigo Centre is a centrally located hostel that caters to budget-conscious travelers. With its affordable dormitory rooms and shared facilities, it offers a comfortable and affordable base for exploring Marseille. The hostel's communal areas provide opportunities for socializing with fellow guests, exchanging travel tips, and forging new friendships.

These hostels in Marseille not only provide cost-effective accommodations but also offer a platform for meeting like-minded travelers from around the world. They create a social environment where you can share experiences, join group activities, and make connections that can enhance your travel experience.

While staying at a hostel, you can take advantage of the communal facilities, such as shared kitchens, common areas, and organized events, which encourage interaction and a sense of community. Additionally, the staff at these hostels are often knowledgeable about the local area and can provide recommendations on sights, activities, and hidden gems to explore.

By choosing a hostel in Marseille, you not only save money on accommodation but also gain access to a vibrant and social environment. Embrace the backpacker spirit, forge new connections, and create lasting memories while experiencing the best that Marseille has to offer.

Emergency Numbers and Healthcare Facilities in Marseille

When visiting Marseille, it's important to be aware of emergency numbers and healthcare facilities in case you require any medical assistance. Here's some information on emergency numbers and healthcare options in Marseille:

Emergency services (Police, Fire, Ambulance)

The emergency number 112 can be dialed from any phone, including mobile phones, to reach the emergency services. When you call this number, your call will be directed to the appropriate service based on your needs, whether it's the police, fire department, or ambulance.

Medical emergencies

In case of a medical emergency, you can dial 15, which connects you to SAMU (Service d'Aide Médicale d'Urgence). SAMU is responsible for providing medical assistance and dispatching ambulances when necessary.

Police

To report any criminal activity or request police assistance, dial 17. This number connects you directly to the police department in Marseille.

Fire Department

If you encounter a fire or need firefighting assistance, dial 18 to reach the fire department.

Hospitals and Medical Centers

Hôpital de la Timone, in the 5th arrondissement, it is one of the largest hospitals in Marseille, offering a wide range of medical services. It offers a wide range of medical services, including emergency care, specialized treatments, surgeries, and consultations. The hospital has various departments and medical specialties to cater to different healthcare needs.

Address: 264 Rue Saint-Pierre, 13385 Marseille Cedex 05.

Hôpital Nord, in the northern part of Marseille, Hôpital Nord is another major hospital serving the city. It is equipped with advanced medical facilities and departments, including emergency services, intensive care units, and specialized medical units. The hospital provides comprehensive medical care and treatments.

Address: Chemin des Bourrely, 13915 Marseille Cedex 20.

Hôpital Européen Marseille, As a private hospital, Hôpital Européen Marseille offers high-quality medical services and treatments. It has modern facilities, experienced medical professionals, and various specialties, ensuring comprehensive healthcare for patients. The hospital provides both emergency and non-emergency medical care.

Address: 6 Rue Désirée Clary, 13003 Marseille.

Clinique Bouchard, a private clinic in Marseille that offers general medical services, consultations, and emergency care. It provides a range of medical specialties and treatments, catering to different healthcare needs. The clinic has a team of doctors, nurses, and medical staff dedicated to providing quality care.

Address: 78 Rue du Rouet, 13008 Marseille.

Pharmacies, can be found throughout the city, and they are identified by a green cross sign. Many pharmacies have extended hours, and some remain open 24/7 on a rotating basis. In case of minor ailments or medication needs, pharmacists can provide advice and assistance.

Health Insurance and Travel Insurance

European Health Insurance Card (EHIC)

If you are an EU citizen, it is recommended to obtain an EHIC, which entitles you to access necessary medical care at the same conditions as locals.

Travel Insurance

It is advisable to have travel insurance that covers medical expenses, including emergency medical treatment, hospitalization, and repatriation.

In case of a medical emergency, dial the appropriate emergency number (112 or 15) to request assistance. If possible, it's helpful to have a basic understanding of the French language or have someone who can assist with translation during the emergency call.

Remember to keep important contact information and documents, such as your health insurance details and emergency contact numbers, easily accessible while traveling in Marseille.

Currency Spent in Marseille

The official currency of Marseille, as well as the rest of France, is the Euro (€). Here's some information about currency and spending in Marseille:

Currency Exchange: It's advisable to exchange your currency for Euros before your trip to Marseille. You can do this at banks, currency exchange offices, or authorized exchange bureaus. Airports and train stations also often have currency exchange services available. Keep in mind that exchange rates and fees may vary, so it's a good idea to compare rates and charges to get the best deal.

ATMs: Marseille has plenty of ATMs (Automated Teller Machines) where you can withdraw Euros using your debit or credit card. ATMs are widely available in the city, including at airports, train stations, banks, and shopping areas. Be sure to inform your bank about your travel plans and check for any associated fees or daily withdrawal limits.

Credit Cards: Credit cards are widely accepted in most establishments in Marseille, including hotels, restaurants, shops, and tourist attractions. Major credit cards like Visa, Mastercard, and American Express are commonly used. It's a good idea to inform your credit card company of your travel plans to avoid any potential issues with card usage. Note that some smaller establishments or markets may prefer cash payments, so it's always handy to carry some Euros with you.

Cash Payments: While credit cards are widely accepted, it's always a good idea to have some cash on hand for small purchases, public transportation, and establishments that may not accept cards. Many businesses in Marseille, especially smaller shops or local markets, may prefer cash payments.

Tipping: Tipping in Marseille follows a similar practice to the rest of France. It is customary to leave a small tip, usually around 5-10% of the total bill, for good service in restaurants, cafes, and bars. Tipping is not obligatory, but it is appreciated. If the service charge is included in the bill (usually indicated as "service compris"), additional tipping is not necessary unless you wish to show extra appreciation for exceptional service.

Remember to notify your bank and credit card company about your travel plans to avoid any issues with card usage or security concerns. It's also a good idea to keep your money and valuables safe and secure while exploring Marseille, using precautions like carrying a money belt or keeping your belongings in a secure bag or pocket.

By being prepared with Euros and having a mix of payment options, you'll be well-equipped to enjoy your time in Marseille and make hassle-free transactions during your stay.

ABOUT THE AUTHOR

SK Travelwitness is a passionate traveler, explorer, and writer with a deep love for discovering the hidden gems of the world. With a keen interest in culture, history, and adventure, SK has embarked on numerous journeys to uncover the secrets of captivating destinations.

Having fallen under the enchanting spell of Marseille, SK was inspired to share his experiences and insights with fellow travelers. Through the book "Marseille Travel Pocket Guide: Experience the Enchantment of Marseille," SK aims to provide a comprehensive guide that allows visitors to immerse themselves in the vibrant spirit of this captivating metropolis.

SK's passion for travel extends beyond mere sightseeing. He believe in the transformative power of travel, encouraging readers to embrace new experiences, connect with locals, and create lasting memories. With the insider tips and recommendations, SK aims to help readers navigate Marseille with ease.

Printed in Great Britain
by Amazon

27461793R00056